Table of Contents

.... 1
Prologue.. 5
The First Message: Questions 9
The Second Message: The Burning.. 12
The Third Message: The Little Sins That Matter 14
The Fourth Message: Atonements and more................................ 16
The Fifth Message: The Scapegoat 19
The Sixth Message: E(scap)ing the landscape?........................... 21
The Seventh Message: Flesh and Blood 23
The Eighth Message: Epilogue.. 25
Some Final Thoughts........... 27
The Day Of Atonement 28
The Sacrifice....................... 30
Adam & Eve....................... 32
Esau & Jacob... 33
Cain 34
The Israelites and Moses.. 35
Timing Is Everything.. 37
Architecture of Purity... 40
Symmetry and Society... 43
Maternal Covenant: Blood, Breath and Beginning..................... 45
Vestments of Responsibility 47
Stones above the Heart.. 48
Gold across the Forehead.. 49
Linen under the Robe.. 50
Bells and Pomegranates: The Sound of Presence 51
Sash: Weave of Calling and Craft.. 52
Oil on the Head, Blood on the Ear, Thumb, and Toe................. 53
Robes in Crisis: Tearing Forbidden, but Removal Allowed.......... 54
Laundry Lists and Cost of Upkeep.. 55
Hand-Me-Downs and Succession 56

Dress-Down Theology 57
Final Seam 58
Table of Fellowship: The Peace Offering's Hidden Architecture... 59
Just Weights and Measures: Economics as Liturgy 61
Blessing and Curse: The Moral Weather System.............................. 62
The Worth of People.. 63
A Currency for the Gig Century... 64
Redemption Pricing and Personal Ambition 65
Compassion as Clause, Not Charity 66
Toward a Theology of Fair Value....................................... 68
Concluding Cadence 69
Instability by Design 70
Public Ritual, Private Frontier 71
Cities of Glass: Modern Echoes 72
The Priests 73

Speaking with The Almighty:
The messages of the Book of Leviticus
(Speaking with The Celestial Guide)

DEDICATION

This book is dedicated to my loving family and friends.

The messages contained within this book are based on reading the Book of Leviticus through a magnifying glass.

The critique (if any) presented here is mine and mine only, and there is no added text from any kind of modern or ancient source which may critique parts of the bible based on different ecclesiastical views.

The passages quoted within this text are taken from the King James Version of the Bible, chosen for being the closest text resembling the original Hebrew version of the Old Testament.

No alterations exist within the ancient text presented here.

Unlike the previous books presented, Genesis and Exodus, this one only contains eight relevant messages.

The reason being that most of the Book of Leviticus contains laws and repetitions already found within the Book of Exodus, which are coherent even to a layman and require no guidance and explanation.

Prologue

Leviticus is called "The Law of Priests", as it discusses mostly religious rules.

But its focus is beyond the physical; it is an array of allegories and metaphors.

In essence and taking away the religious symbolism of it, it is a psychology book into the human psyche, where our individual internal struggles are the smaller parts of the whole - the sanctity of the divine.

Once we reach that ability of being whole, we are to be able to live up to our potential, not as vessels, but as living organisms which can contribute to society as a whole.

As such, the main motif of Leviticus is quite simple: **to think outside of the box.**

Here are a few ideas discussed in the book:

1. Sacrificing as a tool of self-transformation, not as punishment:

The concept is easily defined in Hebrew as "Korban", stemming from "Kirva" that is "proxmity, being near" - in Latin, the concept of "Sacrifice" means "to make holy", but in taking parts, of ourselves, of others and dedicating them to something which we deem holier, is the greatest definition of becoming whole with the world and with others.

In the simplest of terms, the act of sacrificing is a metaphor - we are sacrificing our time and our devotion to be granted a key to something much greater. Something which can only be achieved when we are whole with ourselves, not with something ethereal and untouched.

1. Unholiness and Cleansiness: Not physical, but perceptual and

psychological: We are not dirty physically, but we are preoccupied with so much "dirt" that we must first clean ourselves. That dirt is not necessarily bad or evil thoughts, but ideas which hinder our progress as people, as contributing elements of society. This presents a "block" of energy, if you will, which we must remove by "cleansing" ourselves.

The priests are then Guides, they are there to help us achieve specific milestones and the removal of "lesions" or bad pieces in our garments - are the elements which keep us preoccupied with those same concepts which drive us away from achieving our full potential.

2. *"Ye shall be holy: for I the Lord your God am holy."* (Leviticus 19:2):

This is not a holy decree, but calling onto people to become whole and balanced - a feat achievable by manifesting their best selves. The holiness or sanctity, if you will, in this respect, means that divinity is within - an action must be taken which have a profound meaning.

The moral "code", as mentioned in Leviticus 19, is the core of human integrity: *"Thou shalt not go up and down as a talebearer among thy people"*, *"Thou shalt not avenge, nor bear any grudge against the children of thy people,"* etc. (Leviticus 19:16-18) These words are not a decree in the biblical sense, but all such regulations so people will be able to focus on their own shortcomings to excel in their lives, not focus on pettiness and what keeps them "fragmented".

1. The Sabbath, the holidays, Shemitah (letting the fields rest), etc.:

The Sabbath is not just a holiday for God, but pausing everything we do so we will be able to recharge our batteries. This is the time for self-reflection and manifesting the Celestial Guide within us all.

The Shemitah and the Jubilee are not just rules regarding the agricultural and economic standpoints, but cycled codes of relaxation and giving time to heal. The concept behind them is that we must be able to let go and allow things to run their own course, while we take the necessary steps to achieve them without losing sight of who we are, getting frustrated and quitting.

1. The responsibility of man as a whole:

"If any man of you bring an offering," (Leviticus 1:2) is a passage which teaches us about the free will of man. Though there are rules, regulations and decrees, we do learn that a person must want to do something **willingly**, otherwise it has no meaning. Doing the bare minimum in life bears no results and if there are any - they also, are, **minimal**. This is a message for people to be authentic, manifest their own voice in the process.

When we look at Leviticus this way, we realise that although this book discusses the "biblical code", it is simply a guide for how we may achieve wholeness; that is, how we strive to excel in being the best version of ourselves.

The book teaches us the psychological and existentilal aspects of "conscious sacrifice", not in the sense of letting go but of elevation - the emotional and conscious cleansing, where we connect naturally by releasing ourselves of weights which are pulling us down, where we realise there is a certain plan laid before us, which only becomes a reality if we take proactive action. This is how we transform fears and phobias into unstoppable driving forces, where the concept of temples and tents, is not our reality - but the reality within - sanctify our spirits by believing we can achieve anything we set our minds to.

The First Message: Questions

Enoch: I delved a bit into the book, I see mostly rules here – are you sure you want to go over them?

TCG: I have but one rule: I don't try to explain God's laws or commandments. They should be clear to everyone.

Enoch: And what about the ones which are not clear enough?

TCG: Let it go. Leviticus is based mostly on commandments and laws, and hardly anything else happens in it. It is more of a tutoring book for priests and believers than anything. There is a "repenting" mechanism in place, and how people should approach "God's Work".

For example, Moses commands Aaron to bring forth a sacrifice because God would appear unto the Israelites: *"And he said unto Aaron, Take thee a young calf for a sin offering, and a ram for a burnt offering, without blemish, and offer them before the Lord... And they brought that which Moses commanded before the tabernacle of the congregation... And Moses said, This is the thing which the Lord commanded that ye should do: and the glory of the Lord shall appear unto you."* (Leviticus 9:2-6)

So the entire nation is part of this ritual.

Now pay attention how Aaron would repent the sins of the Israelites not by what they may do, but by sacrifice: *"And Moses said unto Aaron, Go unto the altar, and offer thy sin offering, and thy burnt offering, and make an atonement for thyself, and for the people: and offer the offering of the people, and make an atonement for them; as the Lord commanded."* (Leviticus 9:7)

Enoch: So this is how they repent their sins? By sacrificing animals unto The Lord? The repenting should come from the heart.

TCG: You're right, but this is a learning phase, in which the Israelites learn how to receive the commandments which God had bestowed upon them without asking questions. The Israelites had sinned, no doubt, but Aaron would pay for their sins with his sacrifice.

9

And Moses and Aaron bless the Israelites, with the Presence of God with them, with everyone now looking at the Altar of Redemption laid before them: *"And there came a fire out from before the Lord, and consumed upon the altar the burnt offering and the fat: which when all the people saw, they shouted, and fell on their faces."* (Leviticus 9:24) So God was pleased with their offerings unto him.

Enoch: Sounds more like a message of violence. The consuming fire...doesn't sound appealing to me.

TCG: And you are right, Enoch, but there's a reason for it: *"And Nadab and Abihu, the sons of Aaron, took either of them his censer, and put fire therein, and put incense thereon, and offered strange fire before the Lord, which he commanded them not. And there went out fire from the Lord, and devoured them, and they died before the Lord."* (Leviticus 10:1-2)

Enoch: That's gruesome; why were Aaron's sons "murdered"?

TCG: This part needs to be explained and we have all the clues of what happened there. As you may have noticed, when everything is in accordance with God's instructions, he is pleased and receives the offerings willingly. He pays a lot of attention to details and the order in which the offerings are brought forward.

Moses and Aaron were looking to bring the religious ecstasy of the people.

And what happened to the sons of Aaron? They were watching the spectacle, they saw how the people were enthusiastic about the whole thing and wanted to "upstage" what was laid before them, and with childish foolishness didn't comprehend the situation.

Enoch: What does "strange fire" mean here?

TCG: The Divine Flame is a planned one, in intricate details, what order each offering arrives at The Lord, how the flame is brought forward – the whole deal.

A strange fire though is a "private enterprise", without any specific order; that's having your entrees before you have had your appetisers; it's just something one doesn't do. That is how you worship The Lord – <u>in the Divine Way only</u>.

Enoch: So there's the Divine Way and the Strange Way...so they made a mistake, wasn't it excessive consuming them alive?

TCG: They weren't wrong. It's symbolic just like when the fire consumes the offering and the altar, the strange fire also consumed its own "offerings" as well as the altar.

You are upset because Aaron's children were consumed by the fire. But that is also a "metaphor" as we understand it from Moses' words and clues: *"Then Moses said unto Aaron, This is it that the Lord spake, saying, I will be sanctified in them that come nigh me, and before all the people I will be glorified. And Aaron held his peace."* (Leviticus 10:3)

Enoch: I don't understand; Aaron sanctified with <u>the blood of his own sons?</u>

TCG: No, he sanctified the people with his sons, who were priests and this is how he paid his respects to the people. Aaron no longer had anything to say. Could it be that his own sons were taken by the fire and he doesn't lament for them? Does it seem logical to you? No voice is heard, even if he were shocked by what he just saw? Wouldn't this seem strange to you that Aaron would just **give up** on his own sons?

Enoch: So what had actually happened then?

TCG: Because of their "private enterprise" to The Lord, they were dismissed of their duties as priests, and their own brothers took their place. See that Aaron isn't even mourning, <u>would that make sense to you?</u>

The Second Message: The Burning

Enoch: I couldn't sleep last night; quite the horror story! These are like those all Brother Grimm stories: "Little Red Riding Hood", "Jorinda and Joringel"...What I wanted to ask you though, is in regards to the fact that each chapter we go through, there's something to learn.

TCG: The lesson here doesn't really concern us, but the people who are now becoming a nation. This is part of their reeducation. Understand Enoch, that God's Work was only now part of the daily routine of the Israelites, and its essence was to gather everyone around God and his messenger, Moses.

Enoch: Yes, but what is the lesson to be learnt here?

TCG: The people got what they wanted: the manna, the quail – on a daily basis. They received a whole day in which they may rest, the Sabbath; there is no shortage of water either.

It is now God's turn to ask the people to pledge their allegiance on to him and accept the new laws which he now bestows upon them. They are not required to do anything but "put their trust in The Lord". That requires "obedience" to every Divine whim. And if not, death might be on the table.

Enoch: But that's terrorism, that's fear.

TCG: Yes, but it is required as part of their reeducation as a people. The carrot and the stick here is very clear.

Enoch: How is that good for the Israelites?

TCG: They were given a choice to worship God or other gods, doing what is wrong in the eyes of The Lord; but, instead of smiting them with all his might, God decided to show them clemency and do Moses' bidding by keeping them alive. God is now taking responsibility for the people and is fully immersed in teaching them how to become a nation.

Enoch: And what we, the ones who read these texts written so long ago are to learn?

TCG: I was sure it was clear; we are to learn that one must pay for one's mistakes, sometimes disproportionately to the offence at hand. We must also understand that sometimes we are "powerless" as to what happens to us.

Enoch: Be clever.

TCG: But there's a "bonus" here as well; we must learn how to please the ones who are in control over our lives after we understand that it is the best course of action. That's what "being clever" is all about.

But again, we're digressing.

God speaks lengthly about the least of animals and beasts which are not allowed to be eaten. In case the Israelites don't understand the animal's eating habits or mechanisms, he gives them a least of unclean animals in his eyes.

Some things need to be explained but there is no explanation to them, as commandments they are and must be obeyed. These are the divine laws.

Enoch: And what is the punishment for not keeping these laws?

TCG: Some laws are more lenient than others, allowing one to repent these offences or even recant thoughts that go against this divine dogma; in others, the penalty is death.

Enoch: Such as?

TCG: *"And if any beast, of which ye may eat, die; he that toucheth the carcase thereof shall be unclean until the even. And he that eateth of the carcase of it shall wash his clothes, and be unclean until the even: he also that beareth the carcase of it shall wash his clothes, and be unclean until the even."* (Leviticus 11:39-40)

Enoch: Very mild punishments then.

TCG: We won't be giving grades to God, it's not our place to do so.

And that is the law of what one could eat or couldn't eat, it is important to now understand how dietary laws work in different religions.

The Third Message: The Little Sins That Matter

TCG: I just received an update.

Enoch: What do you mean by "an update"?

TCG: What matters to God is the loyalty and faith in his love. The worst betrayal God may sustain is people who would go and worship other Gods, after he worked so hard to lead these people in becoming a grand nation.

Enoch: That I know, and one could see that clearly. He paves the way for them to go in, and they do as bidding, if they know what's good for them, hehe.

TCG: But there's a flipside to this whole thing.

Enoch: Which is?

TCG: The whole relationship between the Israelites to their friends, themselves, the way they behave, help one another, working together, equality and more. This is part of being human. And that is why there are laws in place, so a civilized society may flourish.

Take a closer look at the Ten Commandments, eight of them are based solely on how people treat one another. These are laws to live by the right way, as people.

These are the sides of this coin: one is the belief and faith in God, and the other is the righteousness of God and Man. One cannot survive without the other, at least now as how God sees it.

Enoch: I think I can agree with you on this one. Because the leader of the people is God, not Moses. Moses is but "a guide", a shepherd who takes the herd to the meadow.

TCG: Impressive, something along those lines, yes.

Enoch: But what is the update?

TCG: How shall I put this...it's not a coin anymore, but a triangle of sorts; the third part bothers God less.

Enoch: No need for any more previews, I want to see the whole thing!

TCG: As long as the offence doesn't hurt anyone, Man or God – it's ok.

Enoch: What do you mean?

TCG: We had spoken about being unclean for touch an animal, or a woman being unclean for a week (PMS) and if a man had slept together with her, he would be unclean and by nighttime of the seventh day, she's clean again (and so is the man).

These offences don't bother God so much, and if they don't bother God, they shouldn't bother clergymen who take unto them what isn't there's to be taken unto.

Enoch: Ok, that makes sense. But isn't there an option of expansion on these rules to include more? Especially when we talk about dietary laws? Would a person be clean by eating an unclean animal as he would be clean had he eaten a clean animal which has recently died?

TCG: One could deduce so, but there is no direct interest from God. So only which was explicitly said as "forbidden" is forbidden. Don't overthink.

Enoch: So everyone who can read the book should understand it.

The Fourth Message: Atonements and more

Enoch: So what is the third side?

TCG: Life itself. Between the laws, the duties and morals, there is the "self". Alone, without interruptions; a lot to meditate, take into consideration, decide and more, at our whim. There is our one chance to actually make a difference.

Enoch: Very poetic.

TCG: We now have the divine reason as to why the sons of Aaron perished; it wasn't godly intended, more of a malfunction. They weren't predictable in their actions and weren't cautious.

Enoch: So you have an answer as to why they were consumed by the fire?

TCG: A clue, of sorts, without admitting the malfunction, post facto. It is said that they ignited a strange fire while they were before The Lord; as in, God was there, doing his own ritual and they entered the "blast zone" and ignited their own fire, and not the divine fire – so they were thus consumed by it.

That is also the reason why God doesn't "let it slide", and just alters the regulations when igniting the fire.

Enoch: I really am shocked by this. I never fully understood what actually happened there.

TCG: That is why the reaction to this was so mellow. God cannot be blamed for the folly of Man. It was clear to all the ones present that the blame was put squarely on Aaron's sons and one should never meddle with God's acts. Each and every offence could be punishable by death: *"And the Lord said unto Moses, Speak unto Aaron thy brother, that he come not at all times into the holy place within the vail before the mercy seat, which is upon the ark; that he die not: for I will appear in the cloud upon the mercy seat."* (Leviticus 16:2) Everything that Aaron should do is to be done with utmost care and caution. The very fact that God might be around, may be dangerous to Man.

Enoch: Yes, very dangerous indeed. What about the term "atonement"?

TCG: And now pay attention, because this is important. We would now learn about the term "scapegoat" and how it came to be. Not all commandments must be explained, but just followed through. But in this case, the explanation is vital for our understanding.

And what is "atonement"?

The people have already witnessed the sacrificial rituals, the eating of the meat, but we must understand that the sacrificial slaughter, despite being an act of violence, provides the people with food as well – not all offerings are wholly consumed, but are also just barbecued meat.

Enoch: This reminds me of the gladiatorial games, in which people were fed while watching others die in the arena.

TCG: Have you no shame, comparing between the word of God and the work of pagans?

Enoch: And what exactly are the people doing? Praying? Nah. They can watch the spectacle, enjoy themselves or skip it altogether. I wouldn't be so sure there was quite a difference between the two.

TCG: You are so judgemental. This is the ancient world, God wishes to unite the people with their love for him, and the need for God to guide them. He is their "fatherly figure". Do you remember when Moses ascended the mountain and the people demanded Aaron to build them a god which would walk before them?

Enoch: How could I forget?!

TCG: Do you remember how Moses actually begged God, to say amongst them? Of course you do. Moses and the people built God a shrine, so he may live among them and they may feel safe. He teaches them what he likes and enjoys the toiling and the sacrifices, the tribute and the joy in doing God's work.

God believes that this is what unites the people of Israel, the fact that they all worship him together and learning his teachings.

Enoch: Yes, but they are not full partners. They don't pray, they don't do anything besides watching his "plays".

TCG: You're saying it like it's a bad thing. These rituals were a big deal back in the day, and the ones they witness are no different than any other people's in the region.

The Fifth Message: The Scapegoat

TCG: Quite the spectacle before us.

Enoch: A traumatising one.

TCG: God needs people's undivided attention, and this is how he gets it.

Enoch: But at what cost?

TCG: Too much you think? Perhaps we should return to the time where they were casting gods out of gold and expected them to bring them to the Promised Land? The insult to God is unbearable, after all, he had done for them.

Enoch: So this is their punishment for not heeding to God's words?

TCG: Not punishment, but a trial by fire – they would now become more loyal to God. They would not be laid astray.

Enoch: I think there are more subtle ways to gain loyalty from people, with more respect.

TCG: Respect? Hah! They are not worthy of respect. They need a nanny, they need to be taught a lesson.

Enoch: Let's agree to disagree. These people had endured four-hundred years of bondage and slavery, they just want to be free.

TCG: Freedom is so overrated; what they need is real leadership, so they may go to "the next level". They asked for themselves a God which would show them the way, literally. But let's continue.

Let's explain the background for this and the instruction as to which animal would be sacrificed unto God, wholly and as atonement for which sins the Israelites may have done. And here come the new instructions, which were never heard before. So that Aaron would put two goats in front of the Tabernacle before God. Aaron is now casting a lot between the goats.

Enoch: What does the casting of the lots actually mean?

TCG: One would be sacrificed unto God to repent the sins of the people, while the other would be sent to the wilderness, with all the atonements of the Israelites on his shoulders.

Enoch: Ok, but what does it mean? In Hebrew, the term is "Sair La'Azazel" ("Goat's kid to Azazel"). Where is that place? What is that place? How is it that the term came to mean "go to hell"?

TCG: You see what happens when you ask so many questions? Everyone understood that if the goat was sent to the wilderness to atone for the sins and offences of the people, then the goat was never to come back as it was going to a bad place.

Enoch: Ok, but still – what is <u>that place?</u>

TCG: A place in the wilderness without roads to reach it, no horizon – a place where you wander off and never return from. Which is exactly where all offences and sins must go.

Enoch: A chasm of sorts?

TCG: One might refer to it in such a way, yes.

Enoch: So what are you trying to tell me?

TCG: "Azazel" is a portmanteau: "Az" (genitive case of "Ez", "goat"; also means "strong" "vigorous" "brave") and "Ael", which means "had gone" (also "ran out of"). So in essence, it means "the goat is gone" as in "will not return".

The Sixth Message: E(scap)ing the landscape?

TCG: *"And the goat shall bear upon him all their iniquities unto a land not inhabited..."* (Leviticus 16:22)

Enoch: But why a goat of all the other animals they had already had?

TCG: The goat is symbolical as to where it is going: to be sacrificed wholly or sent to the wilderness, never to return. Hence the goat is to carry that burden of iniquities and offences upon its shoulders.

Enoch: Ok, but still – why the goat?

TCG: It implies heresy; hence everything that touches it is unclean and is sinful, which is what Aaron had done later to cleanse himself of this uncleanliness: *"And he shall wash his flesh with water in the holy place, and put on his garments, and come forth, atonement for himself, and for the people...And the fat of the sin offering shall he burn upon the altar...for the scapegoat shall wash his clothes, and bathe his flesh in water, and afterward come into the camp...the bullock for the sin offering, and the goat for the sin offering, whose blood was brought in to make atonement in the holy place...and they shall burn in the fire their skins, and their flesh, and their dung."* (Leviticus 16:24-27)

Enoch: Ok, but what does it mean?

TCG: If you'd let me finish, it might be more coherent to you. God also tells unto Moses this: *"And this shall be a statute for ever unto you: that in the seventh month, on the tenth day of the month, ye shall afflict your souls, and do no work at all, whether it be one of your own country, or a stranger that sojourneth among you."* (Leviticus 16:29)

What is this day of atonement, Enoch?

Enoch: Yom Kippur, "The Day of Atonement". A day in which we ask for our sins to be absolved by God.

TCG: And what has changed?

Enoch: In modern times, it's easier – you use a rooster or even give away money to charity, as spinning a live rooster over one's head is very cruel towards the animal.

TCG: True, many instead donate to charity. And God is progressive and goes with the flow of things.

But what's important here is that the stranger amongst us must also follow these rules; but the stranger isn't forced to do so, is he/she?

Enoch: One cannot force others to believe in what one believes.

TCG: *"For on that day shall the priest make an atonement for you, to cleanse you, that ye may be clean from all your sins before the Lord."* (Leviticus 16:30)

On this day, you are not allowed to work and you must meditate and repent your sins before The Lord. It's not that easy.

Enoch: Ok, but how are the goats connected to heresy?

TCG: *"And they shall no more offer their sacrifices unto devils (the original text says "goats", so it is implied that man worshipped goats as gods), after whom they have gone a whoring. This shall be a statute for ever unto them throughout their generations."* (Leviticus 17:7)

The Seventh Message: Flesh and Blood

Enoch: I think I finally got this. The goat here either goes to damnation or to be sacrificed; so unclean as to be cast away from the camp, just as the pagan god is treated.

TCG: Exactly. I have nothing further to say.

Let's continue, shall we?

"What man soever there be of the house of Israel, that killeth an ox, or lamb, or goat, in the camp, or that killeth it out of the camp, And bringeth it not unto the door of the tabernacle of the congregation, to offer an offering unto the Lord before the tabernacle of the Lord; blood shall be imputed unto that man; he hath shed blood; and that man shall be cut off from among his people." (Leviticus 17:3-4)

Enoch: Ok, so let's assume here that a person wants to cook an ox or something, that person has to do it by slaughtering that animal inside the Tabernacle?

TCG: Slaughtering is allowed <u>only inside the Tabernacle</u>. That is where the blood must be shed and treated. You worship and sacrifice for the honour of God, and eat as a family. The difference is the blood, as the blood is the soul of the animal, and you are not allowed to shed blood just like that, not even an animal's.

Generally speaking, it means that a man is not allowed to slaughter his own animals, because then he would be considered a murderer and would be put to them or exiled from his people.

Enoch: So when King Solomon said in Ecclesiastes: *"so that a man hath no preeminence above a beast"* (Ecclesiastes 3:19), as the soul lies within the blood of both man and animal?

TCG: Exactly; King Solomon understood that commandment well.

Enoch: So what are you implying?

TCG: God is saying that the blood is the soul of the person or animal, and he has given the people the altar on which they may absolve their sins. So that the soul of the animal would be used to absolve the sins of the people.

Enoch: I don't think I'm following you.

TCG: Only the altar can absolve one's sins, as the blood on it is the pure soul used for this.

Enoch: Ok, I think I understand it now.

TCG: Do you remember what I told you back in Genesis?

"But flesh with the life thereof, which is the blood thereof, shall ye not eat." (Genesis 9:4)

So God is repeating this mantra, where the blood on the altar washes the sins of the people.

Enoch: I understand it now, thank you.

TCG: Now for the surprise: *"And whatsoever man there be of the children of Israel, or of the strangers that sojourn among you, which hunteth and catcheth any beast or fowl that may be eaten; he shall even pour out the blood thereof, and cover it with dust."* (Leviticus 17:13)

Enoch: So what's the surprise?

TCG: God allows people to eat meat; he is not in favour of becoming vegetarian or vegan. The only term here is that you must cover the blood of the slaughtered animal.

Enoch: And a soul absolves the sins of another one.

TCG: Bingo.

The Eighth Message: Epilogue

Enoch: I have noticed that all these rules are both for the Israelites as well as the strangers among them.

TCG: God understood that the people who wish to live amongst them wanted to be like them, hence the same ruleset or at least that is what God wishes for. But how could one ensure that? I mean, if "cut out of the people" isn't really being cut out of them, as one is a stranger, how would that "hurt" them exactly?

By saying that "every soul" would be unclean, not just the Israelites' but **everyone's.**

Enoch: And then there are the moral codes which one must keep.

TCG: *"And if ye offer a sacrifice of peace offerings unto the Lord, ye shall offer it at your own will.It shall be eaten the same day ye offer it, and on the morrow: and if ought remain until the third day, it shall be burnt in the fire. And if it be eaten at all on the third day, it is abominable; it shall not be accepted."* (Leviticus 19:5-7)

So what is the main reason for this commandment? It is not even religious, but health-conscious. There are no refrigerators and one could not keep the meat fresh in the wilderness for long, so on the third day, you cast it into the fire, to get rid of it and not contaminate others with possible food poisoning.

Enoch: *"And when ye reap the harvest of your land, thou shalt not wholly reap the corners of thy field, neither shalt thou gather the gleanings of thy harvest."* (Leviticus 19:9) This is to ensure that the poor will not go hungry on their way. Another moral law.

TCG: And now God speaks about a boy who is half Israelite and half Egyptian and he has cursed the God of Israel.

What does this tell you?

Enoch: That's his upbringing. He doesn't feel like he belongs amongst the Israelites. He doesn't believe in God.

TCG: This teaches us about tolerance towards others. Even though the punishment for them is a gruesome death. Not because the boy cursed "the God of Israel" but because the boy cursed "God", who is everyone's God and that is something one must never do.

Enoch: Yes, being stoned to death by everyone.

TCG: True, but that's outside the camp.

There are other laws for a person who sheds the blood of another and would be put to death.

A person who kills another person's animal must repay that person with another one (a life for a life).

Enoch: Quite a way to finish the story, hehe.

Some Final Thoughts

Leviticus in itself is a very short book, as it pertains mostly to laws put on the Israelites.

But...what if it was something a lot deeper than just mere laws?

I was tossing and turning in my sleep, trying to figure out if Leviticus had a hidden meaning, because certain events and holidays, which are still celebrated today, such as Yom Kippur (the Day of Atonement), are completely missing from the book, which is taught to be Moses' own invention: Deuteronomy.

The Day Of Atonement

The Day of Atonement, or Yom Kippur in Hebrew, is mentioned in Leviticus 23:27: *"Also on the tenth day of this seventh month there shall be a day of atonement: it shall be an holy convocation unto you; and ye shall afflict your souls, and offer an offering made by fire unto the Lord."*

Oddly, though, it is not mentioned once in Moses' own words in Deuteronomy.

If this holiday is so important, how come Moses does not speak of it <u>even once in **his own book**?</u>

That day was never commemorated in his time.

Not only that, it is not mentioned even once to have been commemorated until Isaiah speaks of it in Isaiah 58:3-11: *"Wherefore have we fasted, say they, and thou seest not? wherefore have we afflicted our soul, and thou takest no knowledge? Behold, in the day of your fast ye find pleasure, and exact all your labours."*

However, nowhere in the prophet's book is it said that he was referring to The Day of Atonement; all we know is that he speaks of fasting.

Judaism in itself has many fasting periods, none of them necessarily discuss the same Day of Atonement which Moses speaks of.

The reason is quite simple, when you think about it at least: It was never commemorated by Moses, which is why he never mentioned it.

Moreover, it was not necessarily commemorated six centuries later, in the time of Isaiah.

If that is the case, then why was it not commemorated?

Moses believed that the event which was relevant for God, that same Day of Atonement, was but a single occurrence and was not to be repeated.

That is why that day is never mentioned anywhere else in the Bible, not in the succeeding book, Numbers, nor in Deuteronomy.

But that, in itself, did not make me flabbergasted much.

I decided to turn to my Guides and ask them for their own theory. I was then very much surprised, as I did not expect it at all. When I asked about the sacrifices, the blood, the gore associated, the Guides said it was all allegorical. That the sacrifice is made within, not with animals or any other kind of commodity, necessarily.

Even when the high priest isolated himself on the holiest of holidays in the inner sanctum within the temple, the devir ("Sanctuary"), also known as the "Holy of Holies", where the Ark of the Covenant was placed, it was symbolic. That chamber may have been a precursor to an anechoic chamber, much like the inner anechoic chamber at Orfield Laboratories in Minneapolis.

That chamber is reported to be so quiet that people who spent but two minutes in it claimed they could hear their bodily functions at work, including their own pulse.

Such a chamber, even if symbolic, may prove to be a concept in which we as people achieve full serenity via meditation, that we can "hear ourselves think." That feat, in itself, could allow us to refocus on energy on things that bring us closer to our goals in life, whatever they may be.

The Sacrifice

The sacrifice, much like the Atonement, is symbolic.

We are the sacrifice.

We do not sacrifice ourselves to the lord; we are sacrificing time and effort to become greater.

This is repurposing our energy where it is much needed, and where we invest very little time in things which bring us nowhere.

Imagine the concept as what Generation Z likes to call "Brainrot."

Brainrot, in its simplest form, is what some may associate with one of the seven deadly sins: Sloth.

The concept here, though, again, does not discuss crime and punishment or good and evil - it discusses not achieving things **we want** by putting our energy where it does not belong.

Whatever that brainrot may be, it is <u>our own fear and overthinking</u>.

It has nothing to do with being called a slacker or not doing well on exams; it also has nothing to do with decompressing after a long day.

It concerns our own fears, which we instilled into ourselves, which prevent us from manifesting our dreams. Those fears are what we like to call "excuses" - the "I will do this tomorrow" or "I might go there next year".

The "if I had the money", "if I weren't this ugly", "if I had the chance, I would -" the regrets associated with it, the ones which keep us up at night, or the ones which bind us to our seats - lead to our own brainrot.

Once we can put those fears behind us, repurpose that energy by saying "Let us do this," we can take our first steps into building a more sustainable future for ourselves by actually achieving those set goals.

This does not mean that we should not be afraid, and there is always a tradeoff: We will lose X for Y, for example: If we decide that we want to be astronauts, what kind of sacrifices in time and effort would we need to make? Who will suffer from our decision to build the next Amazon?

But, that sacrifice cleanses our soul, and the regret associated **with not pursing it**, would eventually lead to our symbolic "destruction".

We see it everyday, when people in their 50s or 60s, decide to leave everything behind and tour the world for two-three years, meditating on some remote island.

This did not happen in a vacuum: <u>They just never did it when they should have</u>.

So, the brainrot is our regret to do something, instilled by our fear of failure. That fear of failure is the ultimate terror: It keeps us well away from our dreams, by associating failure with the embarrassment of ever facing the crowd. It is petrifying, where the mere thought of going after the first dream, can keep some individuals away for decades (if not forever).

But, as mentioned before in "Speaking with the Almighty - Genesis" - God presents individuals with two choices of following after their destinies (dreams, fantasies - whichever we associate it with):

1. Seduction.
2. Forced sacrifice.

The seduction is the one which we see in the likes of Adam and Eve or Jacob and Esau:

Adam & Eve

Eve was well aware of the punishment associated with eating the apple. Despite not hearing the warning when God gave it to Adam, <u>Adam was the one to tell her about it.</u> Adam, thus, was well aware of the warning and still took a bite of the apple. He wanted to fulfil his destiny, as intended by God. It was just easy to blame on Eve, who herself knew what the consequences were.

It was their choice, made by succumbing to their free will to do so, which led them to fulfil the destiny intended for them by God: Work the land, so God could <u>make it rain.</u> Their indecision to ever try the apple, that is the same **fear** of not trying, is what would have made the world barren and less habitable for Mankind.

Esau & Jacob

Jacob was well aware of his brother Esau's birthright. He was the elder of the two, and he knew that Esau would be the one to inherit everything from Isaac, while Jacob remained with the smaller portion.

It was then concocted by Rebecca, their mother, together with the indifference or, more likely - awareness that Jacob was to trick Esau into conceding his birthright to Jacob.

Similarly to the apple, which is not that appealing nor delicious, Esau gave up his birthright for a stew.

Everyone was in on this scam: Rebecca knew Jacob was a crook, much like her brother, Laban (who tricked Jacob into working for him for fourteen years). She also knew Isaac would not be too much distraught about giving his blessing of the elder, that is, the birthright, to Jacob. He remembered very well what kind of family he married into.

Esau was presented with a choice: Slapping his brother for suggesting such a ridiculous offer to waive his birthright and chuckling, or giving it away for the stew.

In both cases, **it was not much of a bargain.**

But did Esau fail in life?

On the contrary!

Despite losing the supposed favour, the fact Esau <u>did not give in to his fears</u> is what led to him being successful.

The next time he and Jacob met, he had hundreds of mercenaries under his employment: What kind of "loser" has that much money to instil fear into his wayward brother, who is, supposedly, "the better one?"

So, what is the forced sacrifice then?

Cain

Cain, despite being the elder and knowing that he should excel, decided not to excel: He brought his offering to God, but not the firstlings as his brother had - that is, the cream of the crop (literally). When God decided to not favour Cain's offering, Cain was mad about the fact God did not accept his offering.

Unlike others, God decided to speak to Cain directly (one of the only instances in which God speaks directly to people, and not through messengers) and tell him that if he excels, he will succeed, and if not - he will be a victim of his own sins. Those "sins" are the same fears of failure which petrify us. Those are the sins which hinder our progress and keep us nested, instead of letting us fly.

Cain, in his anger (still free will), killed his brother. But did Cain fail in life?

On the contrary!

His offspring built the first civilisation on Earth.

That means that God made Cain kill his brother, to excel in life - it was a forced sacrifice.

The Israelites and Moses

Moses' story is even more gruesome: To bring the Israelites out of Egypt after they failed to leave on their own within the first 400 years, and overstayed their welcome by 30 years (430 years in total), God made the Pharaoh eradicate the Israelites. He made Jochebed, Moses' mother, give up her child for him to live in Pharaoh's care.

Moses was then led to kill the Egyptian guard, flee into the desert, marry Zipporah and become a shepherd, only to be then forced by God (as "the burning bush") to fulfil the Israelites' destiny: Fulfil <u>God's promise to Abraham</u> by returning to Canaan.

God then tried the Israelites in the desert for forty long years, in which the greater majority of them (who were mostly non-believers) perished.

But that was God's intention: To convert them into believing the divine is within them, as once they sacrifice their time and effort to strive and reach the divine from within, is when they will unlock their destinies and be able to excel and achieve their dreams.

God knew the Israelites were better than illiterate slaves; he wanted them to excel. But, much like slaves who are conditioned to fear their master (in this case - bondage), they were reluctant to leave and wished to go back to Egypt and into bondage and servitude, not to mention probable torture and the heinous death of traitors.

That is, again, the fear which binds us - the unwillingness to put forth an offering, that sacrifice (not physical, but allegorical) - is what puts us out of harm's way, but tortures us for all eternity with regret.

This is why we have two choices in life to excel:

- We are being seduced into taking that plunge.
- We are being forced into taking that plunge.

Regardless, we have the free will to resist, but that fear will overcome us and turn into regrets, which will then seduce or force us into taking that plunge.

We cannot escape it, but we may postpone it.

Timing Is Everything

Leviticus sits in the camp like a still pool edged by two tempests. Exodus surges with miracles and murmuring; Numbers will march with censuses, complaints and skirmishes. Between them, Leviticus refuses spectacle and insists on structure. It calls Israel to linger long enough for the wilderness dust to settle and hear (beneath the crackle of the distant Sinai thunder), the quieter pulse of covenant life. *"Ye shall be holy: for I the LORD your God am holy."* (Leviticus 19:2)

The command is not a banner waved once at a victory parade; it is a carpenter's rule laid against every beam of community and character. Holiness is measured in the ordinary: the angle of a scale, the gleanings left for the poor, the silence that follows death, the slow healing of leprosy.

Footsteps that outran Egypt must now practise cadence. The very placement of encampments teaches geometry of spirit: tribal banners spread outward, but the Tabernacle draws all eyes inward. Freedom without form would revert to chaos; form without freedom would calcify into oppression. Leviticus holds these opposites in tension, inviting Israel to inhabit the narrow but fertile strip between desert wandering and imperial slavery.

When I read the sacrificial sequences - burnt, meal, peace, sin, trespass - I hear not repetition but the steady breathing of a heart newly transplanted into a body learning its rhythm. Every offering adds one more beat, and the nation tests its pulse against the divine metronome.

Consider the subtle progression: blood first splashed, then sprinkled, then brought within the veil. The journey is inward, not onward. Geography pauses so that intimacy may advance. Whenever the pillar of cloud does rise again, Israel will move as one, limbs aligned to a centre they learned to locate through smoke, silence and the scent of frankincense; this is the conditioning which life gives us: there is a method.

Modern life prizes velocity; Leviticus mistrusts it. The narrative of Nadab and Abihu is not merely punitive - two careless priests consumed for using "strange fire"—it is a warning against unsynchronised zeal. The divine flame descends only when wood is laid *"in order upon the altar"* (Leviticus 1:7) and incense burns at the appointed hour. Timing is theology. A premature spark, like premature speech or premature ambition, can scorch more than it illumines. I once treated fervour as the highest virtue. I was reeducated. Leviticus then teaches us that devotion, if not disciplined by sequence, becomes destructive energy.

The tempo is everywhere. The Day of Atonement allows one entry per year behind the veil. The Sabbath punctuates each week; the sabbatical year releases the land from plough and debt. Jubilee crowns seven sevens (49 years + one extra for leap year) with a clarion of reset. Each ordinance imposes a deliberate pause, compelling the community to breathe in synchrony with creation's own rhythms.

Strangely, this choreography does not stifle freedom; it rescues freedom from frenzy. By insisting on intervals, whether daily, weekly or yearly - Leviticus secures a habitat where worship and work can coexist without either devouring the other.

I have watched enterprises collapse under the weight of continual acceleration, friendships erode through constant availability, and even faith corrode through unrelenting activism. Leviticus whispers another way: build margin - Let altars cool, let fields rest, let lips silence themselves before speaking again.

The commandments are not shackles but governors, calibrated to keep the wheels of life from overheating. When the fire finally falls at the dedication of the Tabernacle, it does so upon an altar ordered, seasoned and waiting—proof that patience can summon power more surely than haste.

Thus, Leviticus, a book which many treat as a legal appendix, turns out to be a treatise on tempo: holiness measured not only in what we do, but in when and how we do it. To those who sprint from miracle to miracle, Leviticus offers a slower drumbeat; to those stalled in fear, it supplies a measured pace forward. Either way, the rhythm is divine, and the next step, if taken within that cadence, will land on holy ground.

Architecture of Purity

How aware were the ancients of our world?

It it often cited that the Greeks, the ancient Indians and the Chinese invented many concepts used in science until today.

The Babylonians were also famous for their astronomical predictions, with which they planned the seeding and harvesting of fields.

Is it possible, then, that the Israelites were of these as well?

I mean, Moses **was an Egyptian prince**, and the pyramids are such a marvel that people still believe they were built by extraterrestrials.

Long before microscopes mapped germs or epidemiology traced vectors, the Torah drew its own map of contagion in the chalk lines of ritual. Skin eruptions, discoloured garments, mould-ridden walls - each is examined, quarantined, scraped or replastered.

Hyssop, cedar, scarlet thread, and a living bird look crude to the clinical eye, yet they form a philosophy of motion: impurity travels. It slips from flesh to fabric, from fabric to stone, and, if unaddressed, will colonise every breath inside the camp. The priest stands at each threshold, diagnosing the exact moment a private stain threatens public air.

Uncleanness here is rarely final; ritual shapes a corridor back to wholeness. When a leper's raw flesh at last closes, two birds tell the story: one offered up, one set free. Life spared is life sent out, altered but unbroken. The healed man shaves, bathes and dresses anew; every layer of the self realigned. Cure must retrace infection's path - outward from skin to cloth to dwelling - declaring that whatever breaks in secret can be mended in sequence.

The dwelling itself undergoes a liturgy of repair. Green or reddish depressions in plaster prompt a careful dismantling: affected stones are lifted, carried beyond the perimeter, and replaced with clean earth.

Should decay persist, the entire house will be unbuilt. Severe, perhaps, yet compassion lies beneath the sternness.

A structure harbouring rot cannot nurture families; its very silence would breed illness. Better a house dismantled than a household hollowed by unseen spores.

What arrests me, though, is the system's stubborn optimism. Every stain invites scrutiny - not to shame the sufferer, but to anticipate recovery. Seven days pass; the priest returns; hope peers beneath fresh plaster. Even mildew is offered a path to redemption. Vigilance wedded to expectation becomes medicine in its own right, teaching that deliberate attention, applied early, can reclaim what seemed doomed. It is rehabilitation before reintegration, transformation secured by paced, visible steps.

Contagion is not merely biological. Resentment, envy, despair - these, too, migrate if unchecked. My own seasons of bitterness and frustration began as small discolourations, tolerated until they darkened the whole interior. The ancient ritual confronts me with an unflinching question: which stones in my life's architecture need prising out before the mould sets deeper?

Quarantine can be merciful when its goal is to return.

The same passage invites reflection on leadership. The priest does not delegate inspection to scribes. He stoops, peers, and decides. Holiness demands proximity to blemish, not distance.

Those who guide communities cannot afford squeamishness about the stains that surface. They must kneel in doorways, assess damage honestly, prescribe slow restoration, and, when rot proves intractable, counsel demolition without sentiment. The role is diagnostic and pastoral at once - a vocation for those willing to smell damp walls and yet believe in renewal.

All this - birds let loose, shaved heads gleaming, houses rebuilt - forms a choreography of hope. Nothing is neutral: walls breathe, clothes remember, skin testifies.

But nothing is beyond repair, either. Impurity migrates; so can holiness. It seeps back through fresh mortar, through laundered cloth, through reconciled flesh, until the camp inhales health again. In that exhalation, I glimpse a theology both uncompromising and profoundly kind.

This is, in essence, the building blocks of our leadership: We must amputate parts in ourselves, that is, concepts which hinder us and make our rest migrate elsewhere. We must have time to heal and for things to run their course, yes, but at the same time, we cannot shut ourselves completely from the world.

Moving forward means making moves, taking those steps forward - we can be silent and not tell everyone what we are going through, or we can, and possibly we will find "a cure" faster. But - we must continue moving forward.

Symmetry and Society

When Galileo theorised that the Earth was the one circling the sun, and the sun itself was revolving around a certain axis, he paraphrased Isaiah when he said *"E pur si muove!"* ("and yet it moves"); the original passage reads: *"The earth shall reel to and fro like a drunkard, and shall be removed like a cottage; and the transgression thereof shall be heavy upon it; and it shall fall, and not rise again."* (Isaiah 24:20)

Isaiah thus discusses that the sins of humanity will make the world implode or, at the very least, collapse with no traces.

However, when we look at it now, knowing that sins are fears, it means that society collapses due to symmetry.

Symmetry in the wild means that all flora and fauna are identical to one another. We know, for a fact, that is not true - the genetic code of any organism in the wild may be similar to its brethren, but not completely the same.

When you look at plants under a microscope, you find out that the veins are not necessarily identical, that there are certain impurities and other qualities.

Once certain organisms achieve symmetry, that is, looking completely alike even at the genetic code, they atrophy and disappear.

The reason this happens is that these organisms have given up on themselves. They no longer wish to evolve, that is, develop certain "impurities".

Not all impurities, then, are necessarily bad.

If a butterfly develops a stronger exoskeleton so predators cannot eat it so easily, or if a queen decides to migrate and build a new colony somewhere else, it is to help society; both of them allow pollination. Their disappearance would mean a catastrophe to the ecosystem, and the need to be replaced by something else, or it would become bleak.

That is the same concept for humans as well.

The lack of evolution, which is either by physical transformation (e.g. eye colour, height, physique) or by intellectual transformation (education, making steps towards building something), will make society bleak.

That is why we must strive to excel in life. Excellence in life is not necessarily becoming the best student or the richest individual on Earth. Excellence in life could mean that we are but vessels to the great success of others.

I mentioned Amazon before; Jeff Bezos' parents invested their lifesavings into Amazon, despite Jeff's own warning that they may lose everything.

MacKenzie Scott, his former wife, invested time and effort in both helping Jeff build his empire as well as giving him the ability to invest his time and effort into building Amazon.

This is not a story of excellence; this is a story of Bezos feeling out of place in his life, in his work, in everything (forced sacrifice) and him convincing his parents and his wife to help him build an empire (sacrifice by seduction).

His parents and MacKenzie were seduced to sacrifice their time, effort and money, so Jeff could achieve great things.

Those great things, in turn, helped both his immediate family, as well as the families of millions of other people, introducing both physical transformation (healthy individuals with a steady income) as well as intellectual transformation (people educating themselves and making moves).

We then learn that society must help itself to achieve **asymmetry**; that is, those "impurities" which show us that this is part of our evolution.

We must not mistake certain problems for impurities, though; those are steps in evolution which never manifested completely, and life tests us more than we expect to be tested.

Regardless, the outcome remains the same: Evolve or disappear.

Maternal Covenant: Blood, Breath and Beginning

A newborn's first gasp rearranges the household's gravity, yet the code requires a new mother to wait - forty days if she bore a son, eighty if a daughter - before approaching the sanctuary (12:2-5). Many fault this as chauvinistic latency, but read it through the wider rhythm of thresholds: childbirth releases blood, the threshold fluid of life, and blood always demands measured reintegration.

The waiting period gives the mother permission to inhabit liminality: no longer carrying the child, not yet re-instated to ordinary worship. In that protected margin, she heals, nourishes, recalibrates.

At culmination, she brings a lamb for a burnt offering and a pigeon for sin. Should funds run thin, two pigeons suffice. The pairing mirrors her dual horizon: one gift ascends whole, declaring gratitude for arrival; the second addresses hidden fault, acknowledging pain left unspoken—perhaps the resentment of labour, the fleeting wish that the crib might stay silent another hour. Neither emotion scandalises the covenant; **both reach the altar by bird-wing.**

In contemporary maternity wards, carbs are counted and oxygen levels charted, yet the mother's psyche often goes unpriced. Forty days of mandated pause could translate into corporate policy: a genuine postpartum sabbatical, graded return, free counselling disguised as "ritual clearance". To skip the waiting is to hurry intimacy, and intimacy rushed tends to fracture.

Levitical pacing lets bond and body knit in synchrony, so when the mother steps through the tabernacle gate, she does so with a joined identity—hers and the child's, distinct yet harmonised.

The rite also reframes community expectations. The congregation sees a woman disappear, not in shame but in protected mystery, then return bearing sacrifice and story. Gossip loses oxygen; reverence grows.

A local parallel might be a civic meal six weeks after birth, where neighbours bring questions, childcare swaps, and gifts calibrated to need rather than Pinterest. The mother's offering is reciprocated by communal offerings, knitting social fibre thicker than any solo resilience plan.

Vestments of Responsibility

Aaron's ephod began with two polished onyx stones, each carved with six tribal names, set in filigreed gold and strapped to the priest's shoulders by blue cords. The design is blunt: leadership must literally feel the collective weight before entering holy space. No algorithm can dilute that pressure; it is tactile, specific, and public. When he stretched to sprinkle blood, the stones tugged, reminding him that every gesture affected twelve pedigrees, not just his own reputation.

Modern parallels need not reproduce the jewellery, but the physics still matters. At one consultancy, I asked partners to pin anonymised client pain-points - print-outs of unresolved tickets, onto felt epaulettes during the quarterly risk review. Ten minutes in, the badges began slipping; people re-pinned them higher, aware of the eyes across the table. Discussion sharpened: "If this falls a third time, perhaps the issue really is sliding off our radar." The tiniest literal weight changed decision velocity more than a dozen slide decks.

Stones above the Heart

The breastplate sat over linen tunics, studded with twelve gems in three rows, each stone calibrated to refract light uniquely: ruby for Reuben, emerald for Levi, sapphire for Issachar, and so on. Visionary decisions pass through coloured lenses; the high priest's chest theatre made the metaphor inescapable. Judgment must consider diversity; one monochrome policy can crack twelve ways.

In product design sprints, we adapt this by ringing the table with twelve coloured mugs bearing customer stories: blue for the visually impaired gamer, green for the environmentally conscious buyer, amber for the time-poor parent. Proposals must line up three mugs and show how the solution shines through each hue without distortion. We have cut features that dazzled investors because the "green" mug dulled to muddy brown once specs were complete. The gem rule saved us from market blind spots.

Gold across the Forehead

A thin plate of pure gold sat on the priest's turban, engraved with "Holiness to the LORD." Elegant but uncomfortable: metal across skin conducts temperature. In a scorching climate, that plate heated quickly, a searing reminder that ethics begins in the mind and can burn if neglected.

I borrowed the idea of digital status bars. Senior engineers who merge to main without peer review receive a five-day "gold band" banner beside their Slack name until the change clears QA. Most days the band is cool; on high-bug weeks it glows, a hot reminder to slow down. Display once, and the wider team internalises the cost of unsanctioned haste - heat on the forehead, visible to all channels.

Linen under the Robe

Scripture notes even the undergarments: fine twined linen breeches "to cover the nakedness" reach from waist to thigh. Modesty is not optional, even under layers unseen by congregants. Transparency in 360-degree feedback sessions relies on a similar unseen fabric - confidential spaces where raw data settles before public discourse.

We introduced anonymous pulse surveys, collated weekly, viewable only by a two-person ethics board; raw comments are distilled into themes before sharing. The breeches ensure exposure serves cleansing, not gossip.

Maintenance matters too. Linen stains easily; priests had to launder garments before reuse. Likewise, leadership attire - mission statements, core values, brand guidelines - must be washed in light of new data. Annual integrity audits drag policy through soapy water, trimming frayed edges. No robe, no value list is self-cleaning.

Bells and Pomegranates: The Sound of Presence

The robe's hem alternated gold bells and crimson pomegranates. As Aaron moved behind the veil, bells announced motion; silence signalled danger. We lack incense-choked chambers, yet remote work creates similar blind corners.

Project management boards use automation to ping a micro-chime into a group chat whenever code deploys or a ticket flips status. The chime is trivial until it stops; then teams ask, "Why did deployment freeze?" It is a cheap bell protecting everyone from the lethal quiet of assumptions.

Pomegranates, fruit carved in yarn, hinted at future harvest while dampening the clatter. Teams likewise need soft additions: rituals of praise woven between hard metrics. We pair each audit notification with a note of gratitude: "Bell: incident closed; Pomegranate: props to Chloe for midnight fix." The alternation moderates noise fatigue, maintaining attentiveness without anxiety.

Sash: Weave of Calling and Craft

The priest's sash combined blue, purple, scarlet and gold threads—colours symbolic of sky, royalty, sacrifice and divinity—twisted into a single band. Identity for leaders is never single-stranded: vocation, competence, sacrifice and spiritual compass overlap.

During inductions, we ask managers to braid four ribbons—vision, skill, cost, and accountability—into a bookmark they keep in their notebook. The tactile exercise forces acknowledgement: if any colour frays, the band fails. A frayed "cost" ribbon means burnout; a frayed "skill" ribbon, incompetence; the bookmark warns before rupture.

Oil on the Head, Blood on the Ear, Thumb, and Toe

Consecration concluded when Moses anointed his garments with fragrant oil and touched blood to his ear, thumb and great toe. Leadership begins by hearing rightly, acting deftly, and walking steadily. In workshops, I invite leaders to identify their dominant sense - listening, doing, pacing - and then mark the weaker two with literal stickers until next review cycle: green dot on earphones if listening is weak, red thumb-cap if execution lags, blue heel-sticker if follow-through falters. The sticky irritant becomes a habit tutor.

Scent matters too. Anointed oil lingered; followers smelled authority before seeing it. Corporate parallels include signature onboarding playlists, seasonal lobby fragrances, distinct typefaces, and brand oils. They must be reserved: over-application anaesthetises noses; brand becomes air freshener. Priestly precedent insists on selective, meaningful aroma.

Robes in Crisis: Tearing Forbidden, but Removal Allowed

In grief or scandal, Israelites tore garments; priests were barred from tearing holy robes lest the symbol fracture (10:6). Leaders should not rip vision statements in public meltdown. Yet Ezekiel shows priests removing turbans during exile to signal lament without desecration. Our crisis protocol mirrors this: suspend tagline from website banner during apology week, switching to a plain logo.

The robe remains whole, but is removed until trust resets. This practice prevented one debacle - when a security flaw emerged, we stripped marketing slogans, issued bare-bones updates, then restored branding post-fix. Integrity stayed intact; trust recovered.

Laundry Lists and Cost of Upkeep

Maintaining vestments drained treasury: dyes, seams, occasional jewel replacement. Hidden costs of leadership mount likewise - coaching, wellness stipends, conflict-resolution hours. We now budget "ephod allowance," 3 % of payroll reserved exclusively for leadership upkeep. Finance first scoffed, then noticed a dip in attrition and litigation.

Launder the robe or pay later.

Hand-Me-Downs and Succession

Priestly robes passed to sons; new high priest received old garments plus fresh oil, honouring continuity without stalling evolution. Succession plans mimic this: outgoing CEO gifts annotated playbook, but successor rewrites margins in new ink. We ask each departing manager to record three "stones" they bore proudly, three "gems" that shifted colour under pressure, and one "bell" that silenced too often. Incoming leader stitches notes into their first-quarter OKRs, wearing history yet tailoring fit.

Dress-Down Theology

Linen trousers beneath couture remind that informality can still carry sacred weight. Casual Friday need not abandon the symbol. A developer championing accessibility dons a T-shirt printed with braille code; a finance analyst leading a carbon audit wears a belt made from recycled bike tyres. Garb remains speech.

The question is: does it broadcast vanity or responsibility?

Final Seam

Garments in Leviticus are not costumes but covenant architecture - wearable treaties between priest, people and Presence. Translate them and boardrooms gain epaulettes of accountability, chest-gems of diversity, forehead plates of public ethos, and hems that jingle honest progress.

Maintenance costs rise, but so does trust equity. Clean linen remains the cheapest strategy for surviving fire, whether altar flame or market volatility.

I fasten my own metaphorical sash, feeling its four-strand tension, and step toward the tent of daily work - my shoulders heavier, my heart brighter, my head tingling with a thin gold line of resolve.

Table of Fellowship: The Peace Offering's Hidden Architecture

Burnt offerings ascend entirely; sin offerings are partially burnt, partially eaten by priests. The **peace offering** (shelem) alone distributes the feast three ways: fat to God, breast and shoulder to priest, remaining meat to the offerer and guests (7:11-21). It is a covenant Thanksgiving served family-style - holy barbecue. Time-sensitive too: meat must vanish by day-two, lest leftovers sour. Holiness cannot be hoarded; it must be consumed in the window of gratitude.

We host corporate victories differently. A product launch lands, and within hours, the slide deck is archived, pizza crusts binned. The peace-offering warns: celebration rushed breeds entitlement; celebration prolonged breeds rot. Better a single evening where teammates, vendors, even failed prototypes are named and toasted—a shared table where gratitude, responsibility, and delight pass in equal portions.

The fatty portions burn first, perfuming the courtyard with an aroma the people never taste. Purpose precedes pleasure: a hint to allocate first dividend to purpose beyond payroll—scholarship fund, carbon offset, pro bono sprint. Only then do priests eat, embodying institutional continuity.

Finally, the offerer's circle partakes, anchoring memory in taste buds and tendons. The modern reading: success should feed mission, sustain infrastructure, and only then satisfy personal appetites. Skip a layer and the fellowship collapses into self-congratulation.

Moreover, anyone ceremonially unclean found nibbling peace-offering meat is *"cut off from his people"* (7:20-21). Joy attracts freeloaders; boundaries keep the feast safe. Organisations need RSVP lists: only contributors or honest well-wishers at the table. The lesson isn't exclusion for its own sake; it's protecting gratitude from cynicism's bacteria, because spoiled thanksgiving becomes nostalgia and nostalgia saps momentum.

Just Weights and Measures: Economics as Liturgy

"Ye shall do no unrighteousness in judgement, in meteyard, in weight, or in measure." (19:35-36) Scales, pipettes, yardsticks - every device the market trusts must echo heaven's equilibrium. In ancient stalls, the vendor's sliding metal stone could quietly tilt, cheating the illiterate. The law slams that fraud not as poor trading, but as profanity: "I am the Lord." Integrity at the counter reflects divine constancy.

Translate to gig platforms: algorithmic surcharges hide in fine print, freelance bids drowned by bot-generated undercuts. Invisible weights shift price and hope. A Levitical retrofit would publish the algorithm, cap margin, and audit outcomes for hidden bias. Each quarter, the platform would metaphorically "recalibrate its stones" before users' eyes.

Smaller ground?

Your own time-sheet. Inflate billable hours to smooth earnings and you insert an unequal stone between labour and wage. The correction is not merely moral but physiological: over-reporting traps you into matching the false number, straining capacity, and shaving sleep. Accurate hours become Sabbath for the nervous system.

The holiness of scale also flips the virtue list: accuracy outranks charity. A fair price paid on time can bless more deeply than an inflated invoice followed by a donation. The shopkeeper who weighs spices precisely does more good than the philanthropist who thrives on hidden mark-ups. Justice in micro-transactions fertilises mercy at scale; skew the weights and every later act of giving drips with unseen debt.

Blessing and Curse: The Moral Weather System

Chapter 26 unfurls a meteorology of obedience: rains in season, peace in the land, barns bursting - then, if covenant cracks, drought, disease, exile. Modern ears flinch at what sounds like cosmic blackmail, yet agricultural societies already lived under weather tyranny. Scripture reframes randomness as relational feedback, turning pagan fate into an educational climate.

Consider personal "weather". Ignore the rest, relationships drizzle resentment; practise generosity, and conversations bloom. We talk of "vibes" - the intangible atmosphere of a home or boardroom. Leviticus names it: blessing or curse.

Neither is magic; **both are compounding returns on small obediences.**

Nationally, the pattern still holds. Environmental degradation marries social unrest. Floodplains paved in concrete flood; rivers stripped of Sabbath overflow. These are not divine temper tantrums but system responses. The text trains me to read news headlines as covenant diagnostics: is the land vomiting out plastics because budgets ignored Jubilee? Are mental health spikes a famine of peace?

The answer is seldom linear, but the questioning posture corrects the modern reflex to treat crises as meteorological accidents.

The passage ends with a curious hope: when the land finally rests because the people are gone, exile becomes Sabbath by proxy (26:34-35). Mercy hides in judgment like seed in winter soil. For modern systems, cease-fires, supply-chain pauses, even recessions, can let ravaged engines cool.

The wise planner weaves mini-exiles—scheduled shutdowns, mandatory vacations—preventing catastrophic Sabbaths later.

The Worth of People

The final chapter of Leviticus lists prices for a life pledged to sanctuary duty: fifty shekels for a man in his prime, thirty for a woman, sliding down to ten for the elderly and five for a child (27:2-7). Modern ears bristle - was it worth so baldly tiered? Yet the tariff assumes the opposite of disposability. A man or woman may vow beyond their strength, then discover harvests failed, dependents multiplied, and the body weakened. They can walk to the priest, speak the truth, and redeem the promise at a published rate. A vow is weighty, but it will not crush.

In Near-Eastern temples, unpaid pledges could end in indenture. Babylonian debtors surrendered children to temple weaving rooms, sometimes for generations. The Torah then interrupts that pipeline: a ceiling on lien, a floor on dignity. The list looks patriarchal; in fact, it handcuffs patriarchy, forbidding open-ended exploitation of zeal.

A Currency for the Gig Century

Transport the principle to today's gig platforms. A coder in Manila quotes $20 an hour; a London client offers $15, citing "exposure". Neither side knows the true exchange. The possible payment per hour factors in the cost accounting of the alternative income for the Manila coder, as well as the tradeoff of giving what that coder deems a discount, just to close the deal. The London client sees this similarly, also receiving quotes from other coders. Each one is fighting to get the best bang for their buck possible for their work/time/effort.

The Invisible algorithms skim margin and seed mistrust. The priestly list would install a transparent conversion table then: skill bands, living-cost multipliers, and automatic grace clauses. Clients could still reward brilliance, but predation would need to hide elsewhere. This then is a precursor to modern actuarial science: Taking into account the cost of living, current medical situation, dependents, possible ailments, and more.

Critics might protest: "Markets find equilibrium without interference." Yet history's curve shows equilibrium tilting toward the powerful unless restrained. Not because the powerful necessarily have better bargaining chips, but because the less powerful are ill-equipped to even challenge the current status quo, not due to lack of finances, but lack of experience in negotiations.

The shekel scale stands exactly where raw barter sags: between desperation that undervalues labour and entitlement that inflates it. It legislates a middle path in which devotion is honoured and poverty is never weaponised. At the same time, universal basic income was always problematic, so this concept tries to upset it to a certain degree.

Redemption Pricing and Personal Ambition

Inside me lives a private market. I auction goals at midnight, then wake to default. A trilogy of half-finished manuscripts, business ideas which begin and end within the same REM cycle, language apps dormant after Lesson Three, gym memberships fossilised in polite reminders - **each a vow outsped by capacity**. The valuation law coaches me: assign cost before making a promise, and if circumstances shift, redeem sensibly rather than abandon in shame.

This is the concept of pivoting, which is often discussed in the likes of "The Lean Startup Method" - any possible upset, that is, a newly added constraint - must be accounted for, so we may achieve our goal(s).

Practically, I now draft three figures beside any new project: shekel of time, shekel of money, shekel of relationship credit. When reality re-negotiates, I approach a modern "priest": mentor, accountant, friend, spouse - state the gap, and convert the pledge. The ensuing result: fewer grand openings, many more quiet completions. Baby steps bring us forward faster than sprinting. Dreams shrink to fit the purse yet still cross the threshold; redeemed ambitions compound rather than decay.

Compassion as Clause, Not Charity

Most radical is verse 8: *"If he be poorer than thy estimation... the priest shall value him."* (Leviticus 27:8) The poor are not squeezed for full tariff; their very poverty becomes part of the calculus. Contrast university fees fixed regardless of income (not factoring in the interest on student loans), or court fines that jail the destitute while merely inconveniencing the affluent. Torah sees equity as a line item, not a sentiment. Mercy is engineered into the invoice. But is it then mercy or clemency? We know for a fact no deed is left unpunished.

That calibrated approach is the book's signature: liability remains, but its weight flexes to the debtor's reach. A mother who cannot afford the post-natal lamb brings *"two turtles, or two young pigeons"* instead (12:8); a leper too poor for the standard re-entry sacrifice presents "one lamb" plus a reduced grain measure - in extreme cases, *"two turtle-doves, or two young pigeons"* and a log of oil (14:21-22). A sinner without silver for a ewe settles with "two turtle-doves, or two young pigeons," and, if even birds lie beyond his purse, *"the tenth part of an ephah of fine flour"* (5:7-11). Fields, likewise, are not gleaned to their edges so the landless may gather without charge (19:9-10); debts sleep every seventh year, and Jubilee overturns generational foreclosure (25:1-28).

Each statute spares the weak from collapse yet still ties restitution to action - wheat measured out, birds surrendered, land left standing. That is mercy: justice re-scaled, never erased. Clemency would dismiss the balance sheet; Leviticus keeps ink in the ledger, but thins the lines until even the poorest hand can sign and walk forward.

If we take this forward, this is the same concept of paying in arrears or erasing debt altogether - the question is: Does it help us?

In boardrooms, I now push for sliding scales: tiered SaaS licences, grants baked into revenue targets, micro-loans forgiven on proof of crisis. Not philanthropy after profit, but compassion at the billing page. Clients notice. Staff breathe easier. And the balance sheet - surprisingly - settles steadier once the friction of unpayable debt is lifted - Just as the priest re-prices a vow to spare the poor without voiding it, sliding scales spare clients without voiding revenue. The debt economy is what societies strive for: Repurpose it so we can reuse it.

Our experiences are our debt; we then repurpose that debt by selling it: we turn it into a convertible bond of sorts, if you will, by taking steps forward and cutting a handsome coupon, much like an investor swaps bonds for equity. That coupon is the milestone achievable, but we also sold that debt to someone else, who takes the coupon (the lesson learned) while we enjoy the new funds received (the lesson taught), and every stakeholder: lender, learner, ledger - **walks away richer, none poorer.**

Toward a Theology of Fair Value

Stand the law on its head and a further insight appears: every life can be priced only because every life is priceless. The shekel table is a symbolic tender, purchasing release from oath, not purchasing the person. It proclaims that service to the holy is voluntary, never enslavement by stealth.

I carry that paradox into negotiations: the contract line item represents hours, yet the worker behind it remains beyond valuation. Pay justly, treat honourably, and you approximate the unpriceable without violating it. Fail, and spreadsheets fatten while culture bleeds. Thus, an ancient appendix turns my daily invoicing into liturgy.

We accumulate certain debt in hours, in effort, in money. What we do with that specific debt, is what matters - do we push it to the limit and achieve a goal, no matter how miniscule, or do we then cave in to fear, in essence - trying to keep both our oath as using the stability of servitude, e.g. steady income, steady life, whichever excuse we make to ourselves.

Concluding Cadence

A leaking body, a redemption tariff, a perpetual hearth: three images that look like scattered footnotes now read as one diagram of covenant life.

1. Threshold tests what spills from the self and asks, "Will this contaminate the camp?"

For example, A sales director, prone to curt midnight emails, now saves drafts until morning and re-reads before sending. The one-step pause keeps fatigue-fuelled tone inside her own inbox, sparing the team from morale-sapping spill-over.

1. Tariff converts a private vow into public cost and asks, "Can the community bear what I promised?"

For example, A local sports club promised new tennis courts, then material costs doubled. Rather than scrap the vow, it resurfaces two courts now, two next year, funded by a transparent $3-per-member rise. The pledge still bites, but only at a weight the community can bear.

1. Fire sets the daily rhythm of removal and renewal and asks, "What habits will keep our shared passion alight?"

For example, a busy restaurant's chef ends each shift with a ten-minute reset: toss leftovers, sanitise boards, lay out tomorrow's mise-en-place. Ash cleared, fuel stacked; staff arrive to clean burners and steady heat rather than yesterday's smoke.

Taken together, they sketch a cardiogram: intake, pressure, release - every beat sustaining corporate holiness.

Instability by Design

We prefer systems we can repair once and forget. The Torah refuses that comfort. Fluids may return, prices are re-scored for age and poverty, ash is swept away each dawn. The camp never reaches a maintenance-free setting because holiness is a relationship, and relationships live by pulse—systole and diastole, give and receive. What felt like endless chores turns out to be the covenant's circulation: stop the chores and the body flatlines.

Public Ritual, Private Frontier

Each motif lifts a private matter into view—bodily health, personal obligation, interior devotion—then processes it in communal space. Exposure, valuation and refuelling all take place at the tent door. This transparency blocks two predators:

- Secret decay that spreads unchallenged, and

- A lurid spectacle that profits from another's shame.

The ritual middle ground guards dignity while keeping empathy alert.

Cities of Glass: Modern Echoes

COVID reminded us why thresholds exist: isolation windows, contact tracing, clear re-entry steps. Freedom requires fences; fences must come with compassion or they turn into cages.

Student-debt jubilees and basic-income trials fumble towards a modern tariff table. Mercy has to be itemised in policy or it dissolves into rhetoric.

Universities, churches and start-ups all struggle with altar-fire discipline. Strategy retreats clear ash, sabbaticals stack hardwood, scholarships provide the night-glow. The motto pinned above my desk reads: "Vision costs. Clean daily."

These finish the meditation, but not the journey. Next come the priests - bodies draped in woven names, heels wet with oil, shoulders bearing remembrance stones. They will unite threshold purity, tariff honesty and altar vigilance in living form.

So I lay down the pen, sweep the ash of argument, and still my tongue-echoing Aaron, who kept silence when the first fire fell (10:3). Tomorrow the anointing oil will run, and words, like fresh linen, must be ready to catch its sheen.

The Priests

The priests mentioned in Leviticus are, essentially, our Guides.

They tell us how to bring forth our offerings, how to sacrifice to God, what it should look and what we should be well aware of.

These all, again, are completely allegorical.

We are taught that God likes the ones who excel, as in: Better do it once perfectly, than do it twice and sluggishly.

We are not taught that, so God scolds us, but that if we do not do our best, our sins (our fears) will rule us for all eternity, and we will be terrified even at the notion of trying again.

That is why the priests were put in the Book of Leviticus: To represent God's intentions to Mankind.

It is not about the actual sacrifice people must make, but about how profound the experience is.

To do one's duty, that is, is not what God intends for us.

We must bring forward all our skills, and we must build an actual, robust milestone plan that is achievable. But we must first accept the divine within ourselves, that is - that free will and the transformation of fears into energy, to fulfil our destinies.

That is how God operates - not in mysterious ways, necessarily, but in clues and cues given to us every single day.

It is then our choice, our free will, to put our fears aside and pursue what is laid in front of us.

For if we do not, we are to let our emotions, that is - our regrets, dictate how we live our lives.

The priests, then, are the allegory to God's messengers, that is, the people placed in our way to show us the right one.

We, then, can heed their words or disregard them completely.

Regardless, these people are neither bad nor good - they are vessels to God's words, and our vassals in becoming the best versions of ourselves.

-FIN-

About the Author

A Romanian-born, Israel-raised storyteller with roots that span continents and a soul that breathes creativity. Father to three extraordinary children, husband, and an artist whose hands find joy in sculpting clay, wielding paintbrushes, and spinning pottery wheels.

These books emerged from a profound life revelation—a whispered wisdom discovered in the quiet moments of retirement, when reflection transforms into inspiration.

Read more at https://celestial-guide.com/.